D0402475

11/02

MESMERIZING

Mind-Bending

PUZZLES

Terry Stickels

Official American Mensa
Puzzle Book

STERLING PUBLISHING CO., INC.
New York

Library of Congress Cataloging-in-Publication Data Available

10 9 8 7 6 5 4 3 2 1

Published by Sterling Publishing Co., Inc.
387 Park Avenue South, New York, NY 10016
Portions of this book are extracted
from the following texts, published by
Pomegranate Communications, Inc., California,:
*Mind-Bending Puzzles 1: A Bundle of Bogglers to
Baffle Your Brain,* © 1998 by Terry Stickels
Mind-Bending Puzzles 4:
Provocative Posers, © 1999 by Terry Stickels.
© 2002 by Terry Stickels
Distributed in Canada by Sterling Publishing
$c/_o$ Canadian Manda Group, One Atlantic Avenue, Suite 105
Toronto, Ontario, Canada M6K 3E7
Distributed in Great Britain by Chrysalis Books
64 Brewery Road, London N7 9NT, England
Distributed in Australia by Capricorn Link (Australia) Pty. Ltd.
P.O. Box 704, Windsor, NSW 2756, Australia

Sterling ISBN 0-8069-8774-X

Contents

Introduction

One of the great pleasures I have as a puzzle writer is receiving mail from puzzle solvers. Your comments, suggestions, and, yes, even criticism, are an excellent barometer of what you enjoy most.

Without doubt, the correspondence points to the fact that most puzzle enthusiasts like a varied mix of word games, math teasers, spatial/visual, and logic puzzles... in other words, a well-rounded collection of any type of brain stumper.

I had two considerations in creating the puzzles in this book. The first was that the puzzles not require specific knowledge in any one area. The other was that none require laborious effort or calculation. There are some very challenging puzzles in this collection, but they require more of an AHA! moment than long equations. First-semester algebra would definitely be an aid in solving some of the puzzles, but it is not a requirement.

So, have some challenging fun by pushing your mind a little further than usual. These puzzles can be solved in numerous ways. It is always fun for me to read how some of you came up with paths I didn't even consider.

Enough writing! Time to play...have fun!

—*Terry Stickels*

PUZZLES

1.

Three dollar bills were exchanged for a certain number of nickels and the same number of dimes. How many nickels were there? Read this puzzle to a group of friends and see how long it takes to come up with the answer. You may be surprised!

 2.

In the multiplication puzzles below, *x*, *y*, and *z* represents different digits. What is the sum of *x*, *y*, and *z*?

$$\begin{array}{r} xy \\ 7 \\ \hline zxx \end{array}$$

 3.

Alex, Ryan, and Steven are sports fans. Each has a different favorite sport among football, baseball, and basketball. Alex does not like basketball; Steven does not like basketball or baseball. Name each person's favorite sport.

 4.

Let's say 26 zips weigh as much as 4 crids and 2 wobs. Also, 8 zips and 2 crids have the same weight as 2 wobs. How many zips have the weight of 1 wob?

5.

Find the hidden phrase or title.

Look U Leap

 6.

There is a certain logic shared by the following four circles. Can you determine the missing number in the last circle?

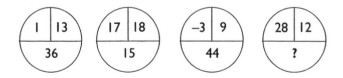

 7.

What is $\frac{1}{2}$ of $\frac{2}{3}$ of $\frac{3}{5}$ of 240 divided by $\frac{1}{2}$?

8.

Find the hidden phrase or title.

 9.

Can you determine the next letter in the following series?

A   C   F   H   K   M   ?

 10.

The three words below can be rearranged into two words that are also three words! Can you decipher this curious puzzle?

the red rows

11.

One of the figures below lacks a common characteristic that the other five figures have. Which one is it and why?

Hint: This does not have to do with right angles or symmetry.

1   2   3

4   5   6

 12.

Find the hidden phrase or title.

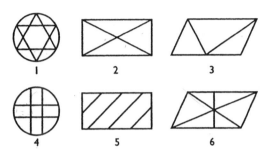

13.

A car travels from point A to point B (a distance of one mile) at 30 miles per hour. How fast would the car have to travel from point B to point C (also a distance of one mile) to average 60 miles per hour for the entire trip?

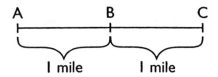

A   B   C

I mile   I mile

 14.

Try your luck at this "trickle-down" puzzle. Starting at the top, change one letter of each succeeding word to arrive at the word at the bottom.

TOOK
_____
_____
_____

BURN

15.

If the length of a rectangle is increased by 25 percent and its width is decreased by 25 percent, what is the percentage of change in its area?

3 1833 04222 5108

16.

A friend has a bag containing two cherry gumdrops and one orange gumdrop. She offers to give you all the gumdrops you want if you can tell her the chances of drawing a cherry gumdrop on the first draw and the orange gumdrops on the second draw. Can you meet your friend's challenge?

 17.

The design on the left is made up of three paper squares of different sizes, one on top of the other. What is the minimum number of squares needed to create the design on the right?

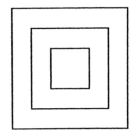 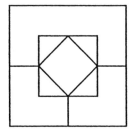

 18.

Here's a variation on an old classic. On what side of the line does the "R" go?

A   B   D   O   P   Q
_____
      C   E   F   G   H   I   J   K   L   M   N

19.

Find the hidden phrase or title.

 20.

Given the initial letters of the missing words, complete this sentence.

There are 100 Y in a C.

 21.

If I tripled one-quarter of a fraction and multiplied it by that fraction, I would get one-twelfth. What is the original fraction?

22.

Two toy rockets are heading directly for each other. One is traveling at 50 miles per hour and the other is traveling at 70 miles per hour. How far apart will these two rockets be one minute before they collide?

 23.

Find the hidden phrase or title.

F R A M E

POC$$KET

G A M E

 24.

Think of five squares that are the same size. In how many ways can these five squares be combined, edge to edge? (No mirror images allowed.)

 25.

What number is four times one-third the number that is one-sixteenth less than three-thirty-seconds?

26.

Below are five words. By adding the same three letters at the beginning of each word, you can come up with five new words. What three letters will do the trick?

Her
Ion
Or
If
To

 27.

If x^2 is larger than 9, which of the following is true?

    a. x is greater than 0.
    b. 0 is greater than x.
    c. x is equal to 0.
    d. x^3 is greater than 0.
    e. There is insufficient information to determine a solution.

 28.

Based on the following information, how many pleezorns does Ahmad Adziz have?

    Molly O'Brien has 22 pleezorns.
    Debbie Reynolds has 28 pleezorns.
    Roberto Montgomery has 34 pleezorns.

29.

What is 10 percent of 90 percent of 80 percent?

 30.

Find the hidden phrase or title.

F R A M E

_____**dance**_____

G A M E

 31.

A mixture of chemicals costs $40 per ton. It is composed of one type of chemical that costs $48 per ton and another type of chemical that costs $36 per ton. In what ratio were these chemicals mixed?

32.

Find the hidden phrase or title.

 33.

How many triangles of any size are in the figure below?

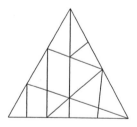

 34.

If the ratio of 5x to 4y is 7 to 8, what is the ratio of 10x to 14y?

35.

Decipher the following cryptogram:

WLA'P XLJAP RLJO XGMXBSAE NSQLOS PGSR GCPXG.

 36.

Find the hidden phrase or title.

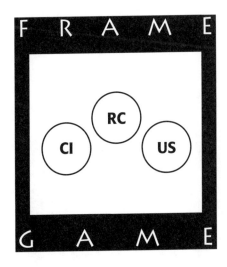

 37.

How many four-letter words can you find in the word "twinkle"? (Try for at least 15.)

 38.

Do this quickly: Write down twelve thousand twelve hundred twenty-two.

39.

Below are four sets of letters that are related in a way known to virtually everyone. Can you find the missing two letters? (*Hint:* Some people have been known to take months to solve this!)

ON
DJ
FM
AM
? ?

 40.

Find the hidden phrase or title.

41.

Find the hidden phrase or title.

 42.

In the strange land of Doubledown the alphabet appears to be hieroglyphics, but it isn't really much different from ours. Below is one of the Doubledown months spelled out. Which month of ours is comparable?

JOKE

 43.

Quickly now, which is larger, 2^{67} or the sum of $2^{66} + 2^{65}$? How about 2^{67} or the sum of $2^{66} + 2^{66}$?

44.

Unscramble this word:

GORNSIMMAROCI

 45.

Given the initial letters of the missing words, complete this sentence.

There is one W on a U.

 46.

Below are six rays. Choosing two of the rays, how many angles of less than 90 degrees can you form? (Angle ACB is less than 90 degrees.)

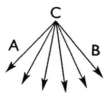

 47.

By arranging all nine integers in a certain order, it is possible to come up with fractions equal to ½, ⅓, ¼, ⅕, ⅙, ⅐, ⅛ and ⅑. See if you can come up with one of these.

Example: $\dfrac{1}{8} = \dfrac{3{,}187}{25{,}496}$

Find the hidden phrase or title.

What are the two missing numbers in the series below?

8, 15, 10, 13, 12, 11, 14, 9, 16, 7, ?, ?

50.

What is the value of **z** in the following problem? (Each number is a positive integer between 0 and 9.)

$$x$$
$$y$$
$$+z$$
$$\overline{xy}$$

51.

Referring back to the last puzzle, where **z** was found to be 9, what is the value of **x**?

$$x$$
$$y$$
$$\underline{+z}$$
$$xy$$

 52.

Most of us know the following rules of divisibility:

A number is divisible by 2 if it ends in an even digit.

A number is divisible by 3 if the sum of its digits is divisible by 3.

Is there such a rule for dividing by 8?

53.

Which one of the following five words doesn't belong with the others, and why?

Pail
Skillet
Knife
Suitcase
Doorbell

54.

If you wrote down all the numbers from 5 to 83, how many times would you write the number 4?

Four of the figures below share a characteristic that the fifth figure doesn't have. Can you determine which figure doesn't go with the others and why?

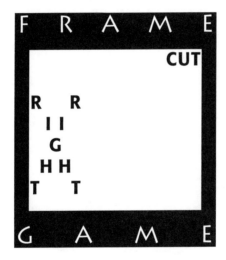

A   B   C   D   E

 56.

Find the hidden phrase or title.

 57.

A certain barrel of candy can be equally divided (without cutting pieces) between five, seven, or thirteen people. What is the least number of pieces of candy the barrel could contain?

58.

Find the hidden phrase or title.

59.

Which is greater, 107 percent of 300 or 50 percent of 600?

60.

What is the value of the following?

$$\frac{1}{3 + \dfrac{1}{3^{1}/_{3}}}$$

61.

The diagram below is the beginning of a "magic square" in which all rows and columns and both diagonals add up to 34. Can you fill in the rest of the numbers?

1	8	13	12
14			
4		16	
15			

 62.

The diagram below can be drawn without lifting your pencil or crossing any other line. Can you do it?

 63.

Imagine that a coin called a "kookla" is equal in value to either 7 gold pieces or 13 silver pieces. If you have 40 kooklas that you want to exchange for both silver and gold pieces and your bank has only 161 gold pieces on hand, how many silver pieces should you expect to receive with the 161 gold pieces?

64.

The two numbers in each box have the same relationship to each other as do the two numbers in every other box. What is the missing number?

| 3, 8 | −5, 24 | 0, −1 | 9, 80 | 6, ? |

 65.

There are six chairs, each of a different color. In how many different ways can these six chairs be arranged in a straight line?

 66.

Find the hidden phrase or title.

67.

Do the numbers 9 and 10 go above or below the line?

1 2	6
3 4 5	7 8

 68.

Find the hidden phrase or title.

 69.

A concept that math students often find difficult to understand is that a negative multiplied by a negative results in a positive (example: –5 × –5 = 25). Can you come up with a real-life example, in words, to illustrate this?

70.

Unscramble the following word:

RGAALEB

 71.

Without using + or – signs, arrange five 8s so that they equal 9.

 72.

How many individual cubes are in the configuration below? (All rows and columns run to completion unless you see them end.)

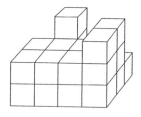

 73.

How many different words can you make from the word "Thanksgiving"? You might be surprised to find how many new words can be made from a word that doesn't contain the letter "e."

 74.

What is $1/10$ divided by $1/2$ divided by $1/5$ times $7/9$?

75.

Find the hidden phrase or title.

 76.

When the proper weights are assigned, this mobile is perfectly balanced. Can you determine the three missing weights?

(*Hint:* Try starting with the 8-foot section of the mobile. Remember that Distance × Weight = Distance × Weight.)

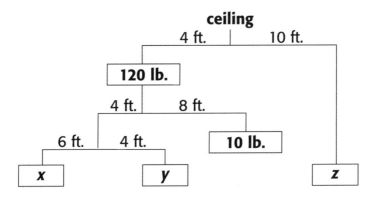

77.

Below are two numbers represented by **x** and **y**.
Regardless of the values of **x** and **y**, all possible
answers resulting from the difference in these two
numbers share one unique characteristic. What is it?

$$\begin{array}{r} xy \\ -yx \\ \hline ?? \end{array}$$

 78.

The perimeter of a square has a value that is two-
thirds of the number representing its square footage.
What is the size of the square?

 79.

Find the hidden phrase or title.

80.

In the game of craps, what are the chances that you will be a winner on your first roll by getting either a 7 or an 11?

 81.

Find the hidden phrase or title.

 82.

Here's another four-letter "trickle-down" puzzle. Find the three missing words, each with only one letter changed from the previous word, to arrive at **BARN**.

M O O D
_____
_____
_____

B A R N

83.

What is the value of T in the following puzzle?

$$A + B = H$$
$$H + P = T$$
$$T + A = F$$
$$B + P + F = 30$$
$$A = 2$$

 84.

If five potatoes and six onions cost $1.22 and six potatoes and five onions cost $1.31, what does an onion cost?

 85.

Find the hidden phrase or title.

86.

Below are 10 matchsticks of equal length. By moving 2 and only 2 matchsticks, can you create 2 squares only, with no leftover matchsticks?

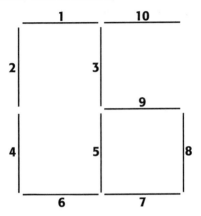

 87.

You've been given $100 and told to buy 100 candles for a party. The first type of candle costs $0.50, the second $5.50, and the third $9.50. You must purchase exactly 100 candles and spend exactly $100. There is just one solution. How many candles of each type are purchased?

88.

Find the missing number in the following series:

$$\frac{5}{12} \quad \frac{1}{3} \quad \frac{1}{4} \quad \frac{1}{6} \quad \frac{1}{12} \quad ?$$

89.

Find the hidden phrase or title.

F R A M E

TABLE
x
TABLE

G A M E

 90.

Given the initial letters of the missing words, complete this sentence: There are 206 B in the H B.

 91.

What is the first number having factors that add up to more than the number itself? (Don't include the number itself as one of the factors.)

 92.

What number is $1/4$ of $1/3$ of $1/6$ of 432, divided by $1/3$?

93.

Find the hidden phrase or title.

FRAME

THOUDEEPGHT

GAME

 94.

One hundred people are applying for a sales position that would require them to sell both golf equipment and athletic shoes. Thirteen of the applicants have no prior experience in sales. Sixty-five of the applicants have previously sold golf equipment, and 78 of the applicants have sold athletic shoes. How many of the applicants have experience in selling both golf equipment and athletic shoes?

 95.

What's the difference between 11 yards square and 11 square yards?

96.

Find the four-letter word that will make new words when added in front of these:

**GUARD
LONG
TIME**

 97.

Find the hidden phrase or title.

 98.

What is the first year after the year 2000 in which the numbers of the year will read the same right-side-up and upside-down? What is the second year in which this will occur? (No fair using digital numerals, like ᄅ!)

99.

H is to one as C is to six as N is to ?

 100.

Find the hidden phrase or title.

 101.

A "perfect" number is a number whose factors add up to the number (not including the number itself). For example:

The factors of 6 are 3, 2, and 1 and 3 + 2 + 1 = 6.

The factors of 28 are 14, 7, 4, 2, and 1 and 14 + 7 + 4 + 2 + 1 = 28.

What are the next two perfect numbers?

102.

What are the chances of flipping a penny four times and getting at least two tails?

 103.

Find the hidden phrase or title.

 104.

Decipher the following cryptogram. Each letter represents another letter in the alphabet.

OTD X GACOT ST BPWF WASFTOOX.

 105.

How many times in a 12-hour period are the hands of a clock directly opposite each other?

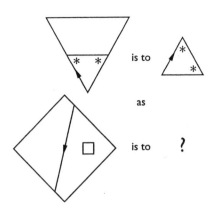

is to

as

is to ?

 107.

A pipe can fill a swimming pool in three hours. A second pipe can fill the pool in two hours. If both pipes are turned on at the same time, how long will it take them to fill the pool?

108.

I am ten years older than my sister. There was a time when I was three times older than she was, and in one year I will be twice as old as she is. What is my age now?

109.

Here's an interesting twist on an old series puzzle. See if you can come up with the missing letter. (*Hint:* This problem is best approached with an even hand.)

T   F   S   E   T   T   F   ?

110.

Find the hidden phrase or title.

F R A M E

CAKE

G A M E

 111.

Two of the following statements are false. What are the
real names of each person?

Susie's last name is Billingsley.
Susie's last name is Jenkins.
Sally's last name is Jenkins.

 112.

Ten men and 8 women can shovel as much snow in 12
days as 8 men and 12 women can shovel in 10 days.
Who are the better workers, men or women, and by
how much?

113.

If you find the correct starting point in the wheel below and move either clockwise or counterclockwise, the letters will spell out a common everyday word. What is the missing letter, and what is the word?

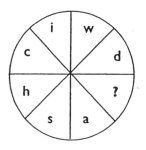

 114.

Find the hidden phrase or title.

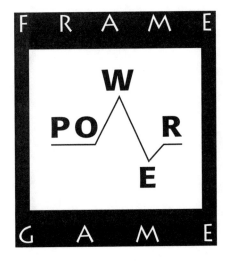

115.

How many digits must be changed in the following
addition problem to make the sum equal 245?

$$89$$
$$16$$
$$+98$$

 116.

In a certain box of candy, the number of caramels is 25
percent of the number of other candies in the box.
What percentage are the caramels of the entire box?

 117.

Find the hidden phrase or title.

118.

Given the initial letters of the missing words, complete the following sentence. (Hint: Think of hydrogen.)

There are 106 E in the P T.

 119.

Change one and only one letter in each successive word to come up with the next word:

R O A D

_____

_____

_____

L O O P

 120.

One of the following diagrams doesn't fit with the others. Which one is it? Why?

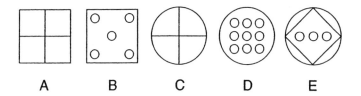

A   B   C   D   E

Here's fun with roman numerals. See if you can match column A to column B.

$\overline{V}$	100
$\overline{M}$	500
$\overline{C}$	1,000
C	5,000
$\overline{L}$	10,000
$\overline{X}$	50,000
$\overline{D}$	100,000
D	500,000
M	1,000,000

122.

Find the hidden phrase or title.

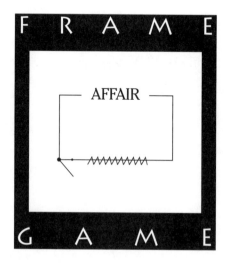

123.

Using only the top row of letters on a typewriter, what is the only 10-letter word that can be created? Remember, the letters are

QWERTYUIOP

 124.

Find the hidden phrase or title.

 125.

In a certain game, a ball can fall through any of 50 holes evenly spaced around a wheel. The chance that a ball would fall into any one particular hole is 1 in 50. What are the chances that 2 balls circling the wheel at the same time would fall into the same hole?

126.

What is the missing number in the following series?

84   12   2   ²/₅   ¹/₁₀   ?

 127.

Find the hidden phrase or title.

 128.

A man spent three-fourths of his money and then lost three-fourths of the remainder. He has $6 left. How much money did he start with?

 129.

Molly and Maggie are Martha's mother's son's wife's daughters. What relation is Martha to Molly and Maggie?

130.

In a foreign language, "rota mena lapy" means large apple tree, "rota firg" means small apple, and "mena mola" means large pineapple. Which word means tree?

 131.

Unscramble the following word:

O M A H G O L R

 132.

See if you can determine a relationship among the following circles to find the missing number in the last circle.

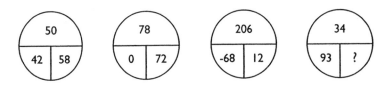

133.

What is the missing number in the following series? (*Hint:* Could the numbers represent something other than quantities?)

13 9 14 4 — 2 5 14 4 9 14 ?

134.

Find the hidden phrase or title.

 135.

What familiar four-letter word can be placed in front of each of the following to form four new words?

Shelf
Worm
Mobile
Mark

 136.

Given the initial letters of the missing words, complete this sentence:

There are 180 D in a T.

137.

In a shuffled deck of 52 playing cards, you alone are picking the cards out of the deck, and the cards are face down. What are the odds of your drawing the Ace, King, Queen, and Jack of spades in succession:

1 chance in 208?
1 chance in 2,704?
1 chance in 7,311,616?
1 chance in 1,000,000,000?

 138.

What number is 4 times $\frac{1}{10}$ the number that is $\frac{1}{10}$ less than $\frac{3}{13}$?

139.

Below is a teeter-totter with a 10-pound weight placed 10 feet to the left of the fulcrum and an 8-pound weight placed 5 feet to the left of the fulcrum. On the right side of the fulcrum is a 14-pound weight that needs to be placed in order to balance the weights on the left side. How many feet from the fulcrum should the 14-pound weight be placed?

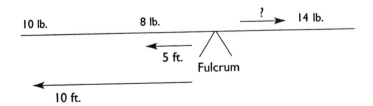

140.

How many different squares (of any size) are in this figure?

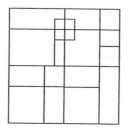

141.

Find the hidden phrase or title.

142.

Decipher the following cryptogram:

SALTS LA ELLG

 143.

Use three moves to get from the first word to the last.

B I K E

_____

_____

_____

M A T H

 144.

The blank at the bottom of the second column below could be filled in by any one of three words. What are these words?

EVIL	**POST**
LIVE	**STOP**
VILE	**TOPS**
VEIL	_____

145.

Here's a series problem that may require a little extra patience...

3   11   20   27   29   23   ?

 146.

Unscramble this word:

A T T R E S P N A R N

 147.

Find the hidden phrase or title.

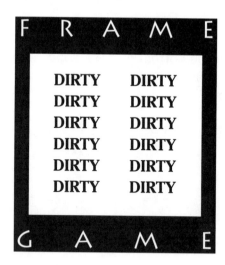

148.

A squash tournament has six rounds of single elimination for its singles competition. This includes the championship match, and there are no byes. How many players are entered when play begins?

 149.

What is the smallest number of square sheets of paper of any size that can be placed over each other to form the pattern below?

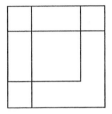

150.

If you built a four-sided pyramid—not counting the bottom as a side—using ping-pong balls, how many balls would be in a pyramid that had seven layers?

151.

Given the initial letters of the missing words, complete the following sentence. (*Hint:* Think of Zorba.)

There are 24 L in the G A.

152.

Find the hidden phrase or title.

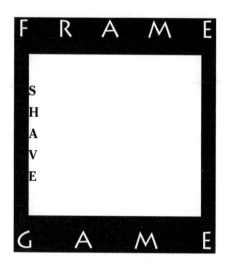

153.

When the proper weights are assigned, the mobile shown here is in perfect balance. What are the four missing weights?

Hint: distance x weight = distance x weight.

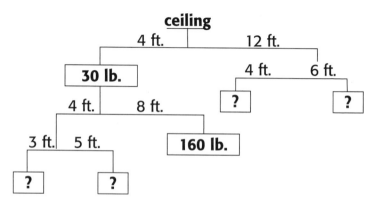

154.

Shown below is the bottom of a pyramid of black circles and white circles. The colors of the circles in each successive row are determined by the colors of the circles in the row below it. Complete the top three rows.

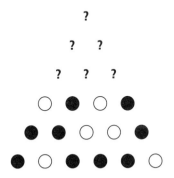

 155.

Find the hidden phrase or title.

156.

Four friends are going to a concert. When they arrive, there are only five seats together left in the theater. The manager will let all four friends in for free if one of them can tell her how many different seating arrangements are possible for four people with five empty seats. All four are let in free. Could you have given the correct answer?

157.

What word can be added to the end of each of the following words to form new words?

MOON
SHOE
MONKEY

158.

In a class of fewer than 30 students, two received a B on a math test, $\frac{1}{7}$ of the class received a C, $\frac{1}{2}$ received a D, and $\frac{1}{4}$ of the class failed the exam. How many students received an A?

159.

Molly can build a fence in two days. Alex can build the same fence in three days. Their younger brother, Steve, can build the fence in six days. If all three worked together, how long would it take to build the fence?

160.

Find the hidden phrase or title.

 161.

How many cubes of any size are in the configuration below? (*Hint:* Think of smaller, easier examples. There is an easily recognizable pattern to this puzzle.)

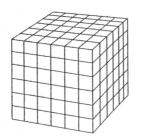

162.

Arrange the numbers in the boxes so that no two consecutive numbers are next to each other (horizontally, vertically, or diagonally).

1	2	
3	4	5
6	7	8
	9	10

163.

If *p* is three-quarters of *q*, *q* is two-thirds of *r*, and *r* is one-half of *s*, what is the ratio of *s* to *p*?

164.

Find the hidden phrase or title.

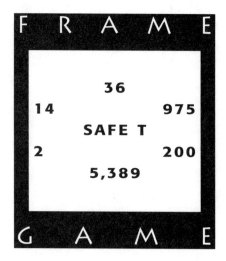

165.

Four baseball players from the same team—Reggie, Chris, Lou, and Leo—play right field, first base, left field, and catcher, but not in that respective order. From the following additional information, determine each player's position:

  a) Reggie hits more homers than the catcher but fewer than the left fielder.

  b) Leo and the left fielder are cousins.

 166.

Find the hidden phrase or title.

 167.

An eagle, an elephant, and a walleye have two. A tiger, a moose, a bear, a turtle, and a snake have one. Humans don't have any. What are we talking about?

168.

Here is a "trickle-down" puzzle. Simply replace one letter per line to arrive at the answer. If you can do it in fewer than the number of moves shown here, so much the better!

B A N D

⸺⸺⸺

⸺⸺⸺

⸺⸺⸺

P I P S

 169.

A bicycle is three times as old as its tires were when the bicycle was as old as the tires are now. What is the ratio of the tires' current age to the bicycle's current age?

 170.

Quick now, which is bigger, 2^{13} or $2^{12} + 2^2$?

 171.

Given the initial letters of the missing words, complete this phrase:

4 S and 7 Y A

Find the hidden phrase or title.

 173.

Here's an alphametic for you:

After Gary had set the table for four people, they immediately sat down to eat. Your mission is to state the exact time they started dinner. Each letter must represent the same digit, and no beginning letter of a word can be zero. Good luck!

$$
\begin{array}{r}
\text{SET} \\
\text{SET} \\
\text{SET} \\
+\ \text{SET} \\
\hline
\text{ATE}
\end{array}
$$

174.

The analogy puzzle below has a different twist. It is a spatial/visual analogy, and the answer is given! How are the Xs in the second grid of each analogy determined?

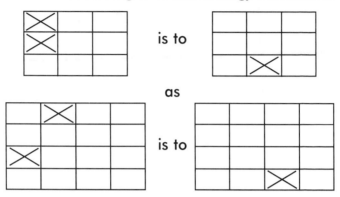

 175.

Find the hidden phrase or title.

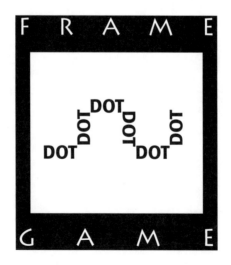

176.

The starting lineup of a baseball team wants a photograph taken with all nine of the players sitting in a row on a bench. One of the ball players wonders how many different arrangements can be made of the order in which they sit. Do you know?

177.

Below, on the left, is a list of words, some of which may be unfamiliar. On the right is a list of related, familiar words. Match the words in the second list to those in the first. Take each word on the left and look for the related words you know for sure. Then think of words that are similar to the ones you don't know—for instance, "potent" is like "potentate"—and then look for a reasonable match!

1. gambol	a. turtle
2. fortissimo	b. hats
3. sortie	c. loud
4. millinery	d. power
5. culinary	e. ambiguous
6. ornithology	f. smell
7. odoriferous	g. refined
8. gustatory	h. opposites
9. humus	i. cooking
10. terrapin	j. cow
11. bovine	k. frolic
12. antipodes	l. raid
13. equivocal	m. soil
14. potentate	n. birds
15. urbane	o. taste

178.

A ladder was standing perfectly upright against a wall. Suddenly the foot of the ladder slid away from the wall and came to a stop 15 feet from the wall. The top of the ladder had moved only one-fifth of the ladder's length before it came to rest firmly on a windowsill. Do you have enough information to calculate the length of the ladder? If so, what is it?

 179.

There are 10 krits in a flig, 6 fligs in a crat, 5 crats in a wirp, and 7 wirps in a nood. What is the number of krits in a nood divided by the number of fligs in a wirp?

 180.

Find the hidden phrase or title.

181.

Find the hidden phrase or title.

 182.

What is 2,444 in Roman Numerals?

 183.

Find the next two numbers in this series.

2 81 6 27 18 9 54 3 ? ?

ANSWERS

1. There were 20 nickels and 20 dimes. To solve this, set up the following equations, where n = nickels and d = dimes:

$$n = d$$
$$.05n + .10d = 3.00$$
$$.05n + .10n = 3.00$$
$$.15n = 3.00$$
$$n = 20$$

2. $x = 5$, $y = 6$, and $z = 4$, so the sum is 15. The variable x can be either 0 or 5. It must be 5 because there is no number that ends in 0 when multiplied by 7 ($y \times 7$, resulting in x). Therefore, a 3 is carried over to the y. Since x is 5, y must be 6 because $7 \times 6 = 42$. Add the 3 that was carried over and you get 45. Therefore, z is 4.

3. It might be helpful to set up a grid as follows:

Alex	x		o
Ryan	o		
Steven	x	o	x

We can see that Ryan must like basketball since neither Alex nor Steven does. Steven does not like basketball or baseball, so he must like football, leaving Alex liking baseball.

4. Seven zips have the weight of 1 wob. The problem can be set up as follows:

$$26z = 4c + 2w$$
$$8z + 2c = 2w$$

Rearranging, we get

$$(1)\ 26z = 4c + 2w$$
$$(2)\ 8z = -2c + 2w$$

Multiply equation (2) by 2 so that the c factor drops out, and combine the two equations:

$$
\begin{array}{rl}
26z = & 4c + 2w \\
16z = & -4c + 4w \\
\hline
42z = & 6w \\
7z = & w
\end{array}
$$

5. Look before you leap.

6. The missing number is 10. The numbers in each circle add up to 50.

7. The answer is 96. Set up the following equations:

$$\tfrac{1}{2} \times \tfrac{2}{3} \times \tfrac{3}{5} = \tfrac{6}{30} = \tfrac{1}{5}$$
$$\tfrac{1}{5} \times 240 = 48$$
$$48 \times \tfrac{1}{2} = 96$$

8. It's the right thing to do.

9. The next letter is P. The differences between letters form the pattern 1, 2, 1, 2, 1, 2…

10. The answer is "three words."

11. Figure 4 is the only one that doesn't contain a triangle.

12. The lesser of two evils.

13. It is impossible to average 60 miles per hour for this trip. At 30 miles per hour, the car would travel one mile in two minutes; at 60 miles per hour, the car would travel two miles in two minutes. So, in order to average 60 mph, the entire trip of two miles would have to be completed in two minutes. But the driver has already used two minutes going from point A to point B; there's not time left to get from point B to point C.

14. Here's one way to solve the puzzle:

TOOK
BOOK
BOON
BORN
BURN

15. 6.25 percent. Remember, length × width = area. Let l = length and w = width. Then

$$l + .25l = 1.25l$$
$$w - .25w = .75w$$
$$1.25l \times .75w = 93.75$$

Finally,

$$100 - 93.75 = 6.25$$

16. The chances are 1 in 3. Here are all the possible draws (C1 = first cherry gumdrop, C2 = second cherry gumdrop, O = orange gumdrop):

First draw	Second draw
C1	C2
C1	O
C2	C1
C2	O
O	C1
O	C2

Among the six possible draws, O appears twice in the second draw column; thus the chances are 2 in 6, or 1 in 3.

17. Five.

18. The "R" goes above the line. The letters above the line are closed with a space inside them.

19. Time slips into the future.

20. There are 100 years in a century.

21. Let x = the fraction. Then:

$$(3 \times \tfrac{1}{4}x) \times x = \tfrac{1}{12}$$
$$\tfrac{3}{4}x^2 = \tfrac{1}{12}$$
$$x^2 = \tfrac{1}{9}$$
$$x = \tfrac{1}{3}$$

22. Two miles. They are actually eating up the distance at 120 miles per hour (50 + 70):

$$\frac{120 \text{ miles}}{60 \text{ minutes}} = \text{two miles in one minute}$$

23. Pocket full of money.

24. They can be combined in 12 different ways.

25. $\tfrac{1}{24}$

$$\frac{3}{32} - \frac{1}{16} = \frac{1}{32}$$

$$4 \times (\frac{1}{3} \times \frac{1}{32}) = \frac{4}{96} \text{ or } \frac{1}{24}$$

26. The letters "mot" will create the words "mother," "motion," "motor," "motif," and "motto."

27. The answer is (e). Remember, x may be a negative number.

28. He would have 20 pleezorns. Count the letters in each name and multiply by 2.

29. $.1 \times .9 \times .8 = .072$

30. Line dance

31. The ratio is 1 to 2. One way to solve this problem is to set up an equation in which x equals the amount of $48 chemical used and y equals the amount of $36 chemical used:

$$48x + 36y = 40(x + y)$$
$$48x + 36y = 40x + 40y$$
$$8x = 4y$$
$$\frac{x}{y} = \frac{1}{2}$$

32. Traffic jam

33. There are 31 triangles.

34. The ratio is 1 to 2. It might help to set up the problem as follows:

$$\frac{5x}{4y} = \frac{7}{8}$$
$$40x = 28y$$
$$10x = 7y$$

Thus, $10x$ to $7y$ is a 1-to-1 relationship. We are asked for the ratio of $10x$ to $14y$; since $14 = 7 \times 2$, we can see that it is a 1-to-2 relationship.

35. Don't count your chickens before they hatch.

36. Three-ring circus

37. Here are 20 four-letter words

twin	wine	lint
kiln	kilt	lent
wink	wilt	like
link	welt	kine
tine	tile	lien
newt	kite	line
went	wile	

38. The answer is 13,222.

$$\begin{array}{r} 12{,}000 \\ +1{,}222 \\ \hline 13{,}222 \end{array}$$

39. JJ. The letters are the initial letters of pairs of month names, starting with October-November.

40. Forward thinking

41. Double-decker sandwich

42. Draw a line as follows and you'll see the answer, June:

43. In the first case, 2^{67} is larger. In the second case, they are equal.

44. Microorganism

45. There is one wheel on a unicycle.

46. Fifteen angles of less than 90 degrees can be formed.

47. Here they are:

$$\frac{1}{2} = \frac{6,729}{13,458}$$

$$\frac{1}{3} = \frac{5,832}{17,496}$$

$$\frac{1}{4} = \frac{4,392}{17,568}$$

$$\frac{1}{5} = \frac{2,769}{13,845}$$

$$\frac{1}{6} = \frac{2,943}{17,658}$$

$$\frac{1}{7} = \frac{2,394}{16,758}$$

$$\frac{1}{8} = \frac{3,187}{25,496}$$

$$\frac{1}{9} = \frac{6,381}{57,429}$$

48. i before e except after c

49. The missing numbers are 18 and 5, respectively. There are actually two separate series of numbers in this puzzle. Look at every other number, beginning first with 8 and then with 15.

50. The value of *z* must be 9 in all cases.

51. The value of *x* is 1. The variable *y* can have any of a number of values, but *x* must always equal 1 and *z* must always equal 9.

52. Yes. A number is divisible by 8 if its last three digits are divisible by 8. Examples: 6,240; 9,184; 15,536.

53. Doorbell. All the rest have handles.

54. You would write it 17 times. Don't forget that there are two 4s in 44!

55. Figure C is the only figure without a straight line.

56. Right cross followed by an uppercut.

57. For these three numbers, 455 is the lowest common denominator.

58. Fill in the blanks.

59. 107 percent of 300 is greater. Because 107 percent is equivalent to 1.07, we have

$$1.07 \times 300 = 321$$
$$.50 \times 600 = 300$$

60. The answer is $^{10}/_{33}$. The problem can be solved as follows:

$$\cfrac{1}{3+\cfrac{1}{3\frac{1}{3}}} = \cfrac{1}{3+\cfrac{1}{\frac{10}{3}}} = \cfrac{1}{3+\cfrac{3}{10}} = \cfrac{1}{\frac{33}{10}} = \frac{10}{33}$$

61.

1	8	13	12
14	11	2	7
4	5	16	9
15	10	3	6

62. Here's one way:

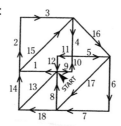

63. You would receive 221 silver pieces. If you were to exchange your kooklas only for gold, it would require 40 × 7 or 280 pieces. But there are only 161 gold pieces, leaving you 119 gold pieces short. The value of silver coins to gold coins is in the ratio of 13 to 7:

$$\frac{13}{7} = \frac{x}{119}$$
$$7x = 1,547$$
$$x = 221$$

64. The missing number is 35. The second number in each box is the square of the first number minus 1.

65. There are 720 possible arrangements. Use the following equation to solve the problem (this is called factorial notation):

$$6! = 6 \times 5 \times 4 \times 3 \times 2 \times 1 = 720$$

66. Hole in one

67. The number 9 goes below the line and the number 10 goes above it—the numbers 1, 2, 6, and 10 are all spelled with three letters; the rest have four or more.

68. Your eyes are bigger than your stomach.

69. Here are two examples:

1. When giving yes and no answers, a person who tells a lie about a lie is telling the truth.

2. Imagine a child rolling his wagon backward down a hill. If you were to film this and run the film backward, you would see the wagon going forward up the hill.

70. Algebra

71. $8 \frac{88}{88}$

72. There are 24 cubes.

73. They say at least 100 words can be made from "Thanksgiving." How many can you find?

74. It is $^7/_9$. The problem can be approached as follows:

$$^1/_{10} + {}^1/_2 + {}^1/_5 = {}^1/_{10} \times 2 \times 5 = 1$$
$$1 \times {}^7/_9 = {}^7/_9$$

75. Elbow grease

76. x, y, and z = 8, 12, and 60 pounds, respectively. Starting with the 8 ft. section.

$$8 \text{ ft.} \times 10 \text{ lbs.} = 80 \text{ ft.-lbs.}$$

To balance, the bottom left part of the mobile must also equal 80 ft.-lbs., so its total weight must be 20 lbs. (4 ft. × 20 lbs. = 80 ft.-lbs.) Therefore,

$$x + y = 20$$
and
$$6x = 4y.$$
So, $y = 20 - x$
and substituting,
$$6x = 4(20 - x)$$
$$6x = 80 - 4x$$
$$10x = 80$$
$$x = 8$$
and therefore,
$$y = 12.$$

Adding the total weights of the left side, we have
$$120 + 10 + 8 + 12 = 150 \text{ lbs.}$$
$$150 \text{ lbs. } 3 \text{ 4 ft.} = 600 \text{ ft.-lbs.}$$

Therefore, the right side must also be 600 ft.-lbs.:
$$10 \text{ ft. } 3 \text{ } z \text{ lbs.} = 600 \text{ ft.-lbs.}$$
$$z = 60$$

77. All answers are divisible by three.

78. The square is 6 feet by 6 feet. To solve this problem, let x represent each side of the square. Then

$$4x = x^2 \times \frac{2}{3}$$
$$12x = 2x^2$$
$$6x = x^2$$
$$x = 6$$

79. Shrinking violets

80. 2 in 9. Because each die has 6 faces, there are 6×6 or 36 possible combinations of numbers. Of these, 6 combinations result in a 7:

6 and 1
1 and 6
5 and 2
2 and 5
4 and 3
3 and 4

And 2 combinations result in an 11:

5 and 6
6 and 5

thus the chances are 8 in 36, or 2 in 9.

81. Calm before the storm

82.

MOOD
MOON
MORN
BORN
BARN

83. T = 15. Since A = 2, we can substitute A into the first four equations to come up with the following:

$$
\begin{aligned}
&(1) \quad 2 + B = H \\
&(2) \quad H + P = T \\
&(3) \quad T + 2 = F \\
&(4) \, B + P + F = 30
\end{aligned}
$$

Now substitute equation (1) into equation (2):

$$(2 + B) + P = T$$

Rearranging, we get

$$B + P = T - 2$$

Substitute this into equation (4):

$$(T - 2) + F = 30$$

Finally, substitute equation (3) into equation (4) and solve for T:

$$
\begin{aligned}
(T - 2) + (T + 2) &= 30 \\
2T &= 30 \\
T &= 15
\end{aligned}
$$

84. An onion costs 7 cents. Set up the equations, with x as potatoes and y as onions:

$$
\begin{aligned}
5x + 6y &= 1.22 \\
6x + 5y &= 1.31
\end{aligned}
$$

Multiply the first equation by 6, the second one by 5:

$$
\begin{aligned}
30x + 36y &= 7.32 \\
30x + 25y &= 6.55
\end{aligned}
$$

Subtract the second equation from the first, and you have:

$$
\begin{aligned}
0x + 11y &= .77 \\
y &= .07
\end{aligned}
$$

85. Rising tide

86. It can be done as follows:

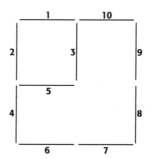

87. Let's have x, y, and z represent three types of candles.

$$x + y + z = 100$$

and

$$.50x + 5.50y + 9.50z = \$100$$

Multiply the first equation by $-.5$, and combine it with the second equation:

$$-.5 - .5y - .5z = -50$$
$$.5x + 5.5y + 9.5z = 100$$

$$5y + 9z = 50$$
$$5y = 50 - 9z$$
$$y = 10 - \frac{9}{5}z$$

Since we're dealing with whole numbers, z must be a whole number and a multiple of 5. In this case z can only equal 5. With any greater number, y will become negative, so $z = 5$, $y = 1$, and thus x must be 94. $(94 \times .50) + (1 \times 5.50) + (5 \times 9.50) = \$100$.

88. The missing number is zero. If you convert each fraction to twelfths, you get the following series:

$$\frac{5}{12} \qquad \frac{4}{12} \qquad \frac{3}{12} \qquad \frac{2}{12} \qquad \frac{1}{12} \qquad 0$$

89. Multiplication tables

90. There are 206 bones in the human body.

91. Factors of the number 12 (6 + 4 + 3 + 2 + 1) add up to 16.

92. 18. $\frac{1}{4}$ of $\frac{1}{3}$ of $\frac{1}{6}$ is $\frac{1}{72}$; $\frac{1}{72}$ of 432 is 6; and 6 divided by $\frac{1}{3}$ is 18.

93. Deep in thought

94. Fifty-six applicants have experience in selling both golf equipment and athletic shoes. Since 13 of the applicants have had no sales experience, we're dealing with 87 people who have some experience. Of the 87 applicants, 65 of them have sold golf equipment, which means that 22 of this group haven't sold golf equipment (87 − 65 = 22). Seventy-eight of the applicants have sold shoes, which means that 9 haven't (87 − 78 = 9). Therefore, we have 9 + 22 or 31 people who could not have sold both—thus, 87 − 31 = 56 people who *have* had experience in selling both.

95. 110 square yards. An area 11 yards square measures 11 yards on each of four sides and therefore has a total of 121 square yards. An area of 11 square yards, if it were square, would be just under 3.32 yards on each side. The difference between the two, then, is found by subtracting 11 square yards from 121 square yards: 110 square yards.

96. Life

97. You are on time.

98. 6009, 6119

99. Seven. These are the elements hydrogen, carbon, and nitrogen with their respective atomic numbers; seven is the atomic number for nitrogen.

100. Can't see the forest for the trees

101. They are 496 and 8,128. The next perfect number after that is 33,550,336!

102. There are 16 possibilities, each having a probability of $^1/_{16}$. There are 6 ways with exactly 2 tails, 4 ways with 3 tails, and 1 way with 4 tails. That's a total of 11 ways out of 16. The chances are 11 in 16.

HHHH	TTTT
HTTT	THHH
HHHT	TTTH
HTHH	THTT
HHTH	TTHT
HHTT	TTHH
HTHT	THTH
HTTH	THHT

103. A break in the action

104. Let a smile be your umbrella.

105. They are directly opposite each other 11 times.

106.

107. It will take 1.2 hours.

The equation can be set up this way:

$$\frac{x}{3} + \frac{x}{2} = 1$$

Multiply by 6:

$$2x + 3x = 6$$
$$5x = 6$$
$$x = \frac{6}{5} = 1.2$$

108. I am 19 years old and my sister is 9.
Let x = my sister's age and y = my age.
$$y = x + 10 \text{ and}$$
$$y + 1 = 2(x + 1)$$
$$y = 2x + 1$$
Substituting this result in our first equation, we have
$$2x + 1 = x + 10$$
$$x = 9$$
so
$$y = 19.$$
When my sister was 5, I was 3 times older than she was.

109. The missing letter is S. These are the first letters of the even numbers when spelled out, beginning with two.

110. Upside-down cake

111. Sally Billingsley and Susie Jenkins are the real names. Because one of the first two statements had to be false, the third statement also had to be false.

112. Women are the better workers. Let's say that in one day, 10 men work at a rate of x and 8 women work at a rate of y.
$$10x + 8y = \tfrac{1}{12} \text{ (one day), or } 12x + 96y = 1$$
Likewise in the second case:
$$8x + 12y = \tfrac{1}{10}, \text{ or } 80x + 120y = 1.$$
Therefore:
$$120x + 96y = 80x + 120y$$
$$5x = 3y$$
Thus, 3 women do the work of 5 men.

113. The missing letter is N; the word is "sandwich."

114. Power surge

115. None. Instead, turn the puzzle upside-down and add:

$$\begin{array}{r} 86 \\ 91 \\ +68 \\ \hline 245 \end{array}$$

116. 20 percent. Say there are 10 caramels. Since the number of caramels is 25 percent of the number of other candies, there must be 40 pieces of candy that aren't caramels. The total number of pieces of candy = 10 + 40 = 50, so $^{10}/_{50} = ^{1}/_{5} = 20$ percent.

117. Fender bender

118. There are 106 elements in the periodic table.

119. Here's one way to solve the puzzle:

ROAD
ROAM
ROOM
LOOM
LOOP

120. Diagram E is the odd one out. The other four are symmetrical about both of their axes: if you turn them 90 degrees, they will look the same as in their original positions.

121.

C	=	100
D	=	500
$\overline{M}$	=	1,000
$\overline{V}$	=	5,000
$\overline{X}$	=	10,000
$\overline{L}$	=	50,000
$\overline{C}$	=	100,000
$\overline{D}$	=	500,000
$\overline{M}$	=	1,000,000

122. Current affair

123. The word "typewriter" is the only word that can be created.

124. Central Intelligence Agency

125. The chances are still 1 in 50.

126. The missing number is $1/30$. The series is constructed as follows:

$$12 = 1/7 \text{ of } 84$$

$$2 = 1/6 \text{ of } 12$$

$$2/5 = 1/5 \text{ of } 2$$

$$1/10 = 1/4 \text{ of } 2/5$$

$$1/30 = 1/3 \text{ of } 1/10$$

127. Guilty beyond a reasonable doubt

128. $96. Use the equation

$$1/4x - (3/4 \times 1/4x) = \$6$$

$$1/4x - 3/16x = \$6$$

Multiply each side by 16:

$$4x - 3x = \$96$$

$$x = \$96$$

129. She is their aunt.

130. "Lapy" means tree. From the first two phrases, "rota" must mean apple. From the third phrase, "mena" must mean large, leaving "lapy" to be tree.

131. Hologram

132. The numbers in each circle add up to 150, so the missing number is 23.

133. The missing number is 7. The numbers have a one-to-one correspondence with the letters of the alphabet, where A = 1, B = 2, C = 3, and so forth. The word spelled out is "mind-bending."

134. No time left on the clock

135. Book

136. There are 180 degrees in a triangle.

137. The chance of drawing the ace of spades is 1 in 52; for the king, 1 in 51; for the queen, 1 in 50; and for the jack, 1 in 49. To calculate the answer, multiply these altogether:

$$\tfrac{1}{52} \times \tfrac{1}{51} \times \tfrac{1}{50} \times \tfrac{1}{49} = \tfrac{1}{6,497,400}$$

138.

$^{34}/_{650}$ or $^{17}/_{325}$

$^{1}/_{10}$ less than $^{3}/_{13}$ is:

$^{30}/_{130} - {}^{13}/_{130} = {}^{17}/_{130}$

4 times $^{1}/_{10}$ of that number is:

$$4 \times \tfrac{1}{10} \times {}^{17}/_{130} = {}^{4}/_{10} \times {}^{17}/_{130}$$
$$= \tfrac{2}{5} \times {}^{17}/_{130}$$
$$= {}^{34}/_{650}$$
$$= {}^{17}/_{325}$$

139. The weight should be placed 10 feet from the fulcrum. To solve this, first calculate foot-pounds (a unit of work combining force and distance) on the left side:

$$(5 \text{ ft.} \times 8 \text{ lbs.}) + (10 \text{ ft.} \times 10 \text{ lbs.}) = 140 \text{ ft.-lbs.}$$

The right side must equal the left side:

$$x \text{ ft.} \times 14 \text{ lbs.} = 140 \text{ ft.-lbs.}$$

Solving for x; we get

$$x = {}^{140}/_{14} = 10$$

140. There are 19 squares.

141. Slim chance

142. Knock on wood.

143.

> BIKE
> BITE
> MITE
> MATE
> MATH

144. POTS, SPOT, and OPTS. These are the only three remaining four-letter words that can be made by using the letters O, P, S, and T only once.

145. The missing number is 6. Keep taking the differences between numbers (keeping in mind positive and negative differences) and you get:

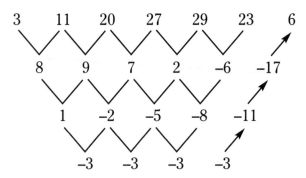

146. Transparent

147. Dirty dozen

148. With players for each match through six rounds, 2^6 or 64 players are entered.

149. Five. Square 1 is the largest square and frames the whole figure. Then square 2 is placed in the lower right corner, and square 3 is placed in the upper left corner. (Square 2 and square 3 are the same size.) Square 4 is placed over square 3 in the upper-left corner, and square 5 is placed in the middle.

150. Each layer would contain a number of balls equal to the square of the layer. In other words, layer 1 (the top layer) would have $1^2 = 1$ ball; layer 2 would have $2^2 = 4$ balls; layer 3 would have $3^2 = 9$ balls; and so on. The layers would stack up like this, for a total of 140 balls.

$$\begin{array}{r} 1 \\ 4 \\ 6 \\ 25 \\ 36 \\ \underline{49} \\ 140 \end{array}$$

151. There are 24 letters in the Greek alphabet.

152. Close shave

153. From left to right, the weights are 200 lbs., 120 lbs., 102 lbs., and 68 lbs.

First we find the two weights on the left. Their total weight (call it a) at a distance of 4 ft must balance 160 lbs. at a distance of 8 ft:

$$4a = 8 \times 160$$
$$a = 1{,}280 \div 4 = 320 \text{ lbs.}$$

Then $5/8$ of this weight at 3 ft must balance $3/8$ of this weight at 5 ft:

$$\frac{5}{8} \times 320 = 200 \text{ lbs. and } \frac{3}{8} \times 320 = 120 \text{ lbs.}$$

Next we find the two weights on the right. Their total weight (call it b) at a distance of 12 ft must balance 200 + 120 + 160 + 30 = 510 lbs. at a distance of 4 ft:

$$12b = 4 \times 510$$
$$b = 2040 \div 12 = 170 \text{ lbs.}$$

Then $6/10$ of this weight at 4 ft must balance $4/10$ of this weight at 6 ft:

$$\frac{6}{10} \times 170 = 102 \text{ lbs. and } \frac{4}{10} \times 170 = 68 \text{ lbs.}$$

154. Starting with the bottom row, determine if two adjacent circles are different colors. A black circle goes above and between different-colored circles. A white circle goes above and between same-colored circles. The top of the pyramid is shown below.

155. The proof is in the pudding.

156. Four people can sit in five seats as follows:
$5 \times 4 \times 3 \times 2$, for a total of 120 different ways.

157. Shine

158. The best approach to this problem is to find a common denominator of 2, 4, and 7 that is less than 30—that is 28. Then add up the calculated numbers of students:

2 students received a B

¼ of 28 = 7 students failed

½ of 28 = 14 students received a D

⅐ of 28 = 4 students received a C

totalling 27, which means only 1 student received an A.

159. 1 day. Let x be the number of days it would take all three to build the fence. In 1 day the total of their individual contributions to building the fence would be:

$$\frac{x}{2} + \frac{x}{3} + \frac{x}{6} = 1$$
$$\frac{3x}{6} + \frac{2x}{6} + \frac{x}{6} = \frac{6}{6}$$
$$6x = 6$$
$$x = 1 \text{ day}$$

160. Foreign correspondent

161. 441. Use the following formula to find the number of cubes when the width, length, and height of the stack have the same number of cubes.

Let c = that number of cubes.

$$c^3 + (c-1)^3 = (c-2)^3 = (c-3)^3 \ldots (c-c)^3$$

So,

$$6^3 + 5^3 + 4^3 + 3^3 + 2^3 + 1^3 =$$
$$216 + 125 + 64 + 27 + 8 + 1 = 441$$
total cubes.

162. Here's one way. Can you find others?

2	10	
5	8	6
3	1	4
	9	7

163. 4 to 1. Here is one way to solve this:

if $p = \frac{3}{4}q$, then $q = \frac{4}{3}p$

if $q = \frac{2}{3}r$, then $r = \frac{3}{2}q$ and

if $r = \frac{1}{2}s$, then $s = \frac{2}{1}r$

Therefore,

$$s \text{ to } p \text{ is } \frac{2}{1} \times \frac{3}{2} \times \frac{4}{3} = \frac{24}{6} = 4 \text{ to } 1$$

164. Safety in numbers

165.   first base: Reggie
             catcher: Lou
             right field: Leo
             left field: Chris

Here's how to deduce the answer from the given facts:

Reggie: From the question we know that Reggie can't play right field. From point (a) we know that Reggie isn't the catcher or the left fielder, so he must be the first baseman.

Leo: From the question we know that Leo can't be the catcher, and from point (b) we know that Leo can't be the left fielder. He can't play first base because that's Reggie's position, so he must be the right fielder.

Lou: From the question we know that Lou can't play left field. He can't play first base (Reggie's position) or right field (Leo's position), so he must be the catcher.

Chris: With all the other positions filled, Chris must be the left fielder.

166. Golden anniversary

167. The letter e.

168.
             BAND
             BIND
             BINS
             PINS
             PIPS

169. 2 to 3. Let the bicycle's current age be $3x$ making the tires' age x when the bicycle was old as the tires are now. To make them the same age we must add to the tires' age some number, y, and subtract from the bicycle's age the same number, y:

$$\underline{\text{bike's age} \quad \text{tires' age}}$$
$$2x - y = x + y$$
$$2x = 2y$$
$$x = y$$

Since we've already established that $x = y$, we can substitute y for x in the bike's current age:

$$3x = 3y$$

The tires' current age is then $2y$, and the ratio of the tires' current age to the bicycle's current age is $2y/3y$, a ratio of 2 to 3.

170.

$$2^{13}, \text{ by a lot}$$
$$2^{13} = 8,192$$
$$\text{but}$$
$$2^{12} + 2^{2} = 4,096 + 4 = 4,100$$

171. Four score and seven years ago

172. Repeating rifles

173. 7:28

$$
\begin{array}{r}
182 \\
182 \\
182 \\
+182 \\
\hline
728
\end{array}
$$

174. Number the grids as shown below, designating the row and column of each box. The sum of the numbers in the marked boxes in the first grids (11 + 21 and 12 + 31) equal the numbers in the marked boxes in the second grids (32 and 43, respectively).

11	12	13
21	22	23
31	32	33

11	12	13	14
21	22	23	24
31	32	33	34
41	42	43	44

175. Connect the dots

176. $9 \times 8 \times 7 \times 6 \times 5 \times 4 \times 3 \times 2 \times 1 = 362,880$ different seating arrangements. In mathematics, this is written "9!" and called "factorial 9."

177.

1. gambol	k.	frolic
2. fortissimo	c.	loud
3. sortie	l.	raid
4. millinery	b.	hats
5. culinary	i.	cooking
6. ornithology	n.	birds
7. odoriferous	f.	smell
8. gustatory	o.	taste
9. humus	m.	soil
10. terrapin	a.	turtle
11. bovine	j.	cow
12. antipodes	h.	opposites
13. equivocal	e.	ambiguous
14. potentate	d.	power
15. urbane	g.	refined

178. There is sufficient information. The ladder is 25 feet long. A diagram helps in the solution:

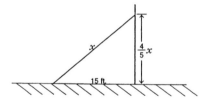

The ladder leaning against the wall makes a triangle. Let's call the ladder's length x. Since the top slid down to a point four-fifths of the ladder's length up the wall, we know that that side is $\frac{4}{5}x$. The base of the triangle is 15 feet, which is the distance the foot of the ladder slid along the ground. Using the Pythagorean theorem ($c2 = a2 + b2$), we can find the length of the ladder:

$$x^2 = \left(\frac{4}{5}x\right)^2 + 225 \qquad\qquad 25x^2 = 16x^2 + 5625$$
$$\qquad\qquad\qquad\qquad\qquad 9x^2 = 5625$$
$$x^2 = \frac{16}{25}x^2 + 225 \qquad\qquad x^2 = 625$$
$$\qquad\qquad\qquad\qquad\qquad x = 25 \text{ ft.}$$

179. 70

$$1f = 10k$$
$$1c = 6f = 6 \times 10k = 60k$$
$$1w = 5c = 5 \times 60k = 300k$$
$$1n = 7w = 7 \times 300k = 2100k$$

Thus, there are 2100 krits in a nood. We also see that

$$1w = 300k = 30(10k) = 30f$$

Therefore, there are 30 fligs in a wirp.

180. Two wrongs don't make a right.

181. Out to lunch

182. MMXDXLIV

183. 162. 1. Starting at left, every other number is multiplied by 3. Starting at right, every other number is also multiplied by 3.

Index

Note: Answer page numbers are in italics.

WHAT IS AMERICAN MENSA?

AMERICAN MENSA
The High IQ Society

One out of 50 people qualifies
for American Mensa …
Are YOU the One?

American Mensa, Ltd. is an organization for individuals who have one common trait: a score in the top two percent of the population on a standardized intelligence test. Over five million Americans are eligible for membership … you may be one of them.

Looking for intellectual stimulation?

You'll find a good "mental workout" in the Mensa Bulletin, our national magazine. Voice your opinion in the newsletter published by your local group. And attend activities and gatherings with fascinating programs and engaging conversation.

Looking for social interaction?

There's something happening on the Mensa calendar almost daily. These range from lectures to game nights to parties. Each year, there are over 40 regional gatherings and the Annual Gathering, where you can meet people, exchange ideas, and make interesting new friends.

LOOKING FOR OTHERS
WHO SHARE YOUR SPECIAL INTEREST?

Whether your interest might be computer gaming, the meaning of life, science fiction & fantasy, or scuba diving, there's probably a Mensa Special Interest Group (SIG) for you. There are over 150 SIGs, maintained by members just in the United States.

So visit our Web site for more information about American Mensa Ltd.

http://www.us.mensa.org

Or call our automated messaging system to request an application or for additional information:

(800) 66-MENSA

Or write to us at:

**American Mensa Ltd.
1229 Corporate Drive West
Arlington, TX 76006**

AmericanMensa@mensa.org

If you don't live in the United States and would like to get in touch with your national Mensa organization, contact:

**Mensa International
15 The Ivories
6–8 Northampton Street, Islington
London N1 2HY England**

---

www.mensa.org